Thoughts of A Wounded Healer

By

Connie Howell

LAFAYETTE, TENNESSEE
deepreadpress@gmail.com

First Edition

Published in the United States of America

Edited by: Constance Laswell

Cover Design by: Kim Gammon

ISBN: 978-1-954989-35-1

DEEP READ PRESS

Lafayette, Tennessee

www.deepreadpress.com

deepreadpress@gmail.com

For

Lovers of deep thought and poetic expression
And
For wounded healers everywhere

A Wounded Healer

I am a wounded healer.
My life has been my quest.
Just like the hero's journey
It's often been a test.

I've stumbled and I've fallen
Having tried to do my best.
The road was hard and tiring
But there were times that I could rest.

I am a wounded healer.
It's made me whole and strong.
Along the way I learned that
I really do belong.

Mistake

I made a big mistake today.
It really was quite bad.
I'd hoped I could do better
So, it made me feel quite sad.
But what I learned about myself
Is that I am only human.
And if I make another one
Instead of just assuming
That I'm bad, flawed and tardy,
I'll remind myself that
I will get through.
For my spirit is quite hardy.

The Mirror

I looked into the mirror.
I didn't like what I could see.
No matter how I stared
It didn't look like me.
Inside my head I'm twenty
My mind just can't compute.
The face with lines a plenty
Is somehow mine to keep.
I look again much harder
And decide I need to sleep.
Then maybe that old mirror
Will reflect a face I like
And if it shows the same thing
Then it can take a hike.
Problem solved.

Alone

Who would I be without you?
A person, separate and complete.
Or am I half of a whole?
Can I be other than I am?
When I'm with you
Will I survive if you are gone?
How would life be different?
Would I choose to go on?
Alone, bereft for my other self.
My heart cries out at the thought of loss
I worry that it won't recover,
If you are gone

The Empty House

The empty house stood solemn and forlorn.
Neglected rooms where people once lived.
Where people had died, and some were born.
Rich memories stuck in empty spaces.
The ghosts of men and women's faces
No one to bear witness to the forgotten history.
Their lives remain an unsolved mystery.
As the living scurry by not wanting to know
The names, the loves, the ups and downs
Of the residents long ago

The Eagle

Her wings are powerful, her eyes are sharp
She circles, watching alert and bright.
What majesty in motion, a pure delight
To see her in her kingdom.

Her talons ready to snatch her prey,
The moment it's in sight.
Unguarded against the mighty bird
All it can do is run and hide.

I want the eagle to have her meal,
But I am sorry for the life she'll take.
The prey itself eats other creatures,
It is hard to see life feeding on life.

Young and Old

When I was young, I played a lot,
I didn't have a worry.
But as I grew, I only knew.
That life held lots of sorrow.
I did my best to let them rest
But nightmares came to haunt me.
And now I'm old, I've grown quite bold.
I know that dreams can't hurt me.

The child is still inside me.
She lets me know she's there.
She doesn't have a worry.
She doesn't have a care,
I leave her to her playing
While the older me takes charge
Of daily chores and living.
The child is happy playing
In the freedom that she feels.

The Darkness

Can you hear me I shout.
Nothing, no reply, no sound
I call again.
Is anyone there?
Can you hear me?
Please answer.

The dark casts shadowy forms
Are they real or imaginary?
Don't hurt me I say.
Then I realise that it is my fear
That keeps the light from me.

I start to panic, I feel alone,
I'm in the dark, I can't see.
I don't know where I am.
There is no one to help me.

It's futile but I shout once more,
Hoping, wishing someone would come.
To rescue me from my aloneness,
But no one comes so
I fall into the shadows.
No point in calling out.
I'm no longer there.

A Busy Mind

Thoughts echo in my head,
I meditate to find silence instead.
Of the constant chatter.
The incessant talk will not stop,
And try as I may, I cannot drop
Into the calm quiet void.
The same old thoughts go round and round.
On an endless loop of shaky ground.
Over and over the same old talk
Like the sound of chalk
Being scraped on the board at school
I remind myself that I'm a fool.
Caught, in this cycle.
Of endless thought

The Butcher Bird

I wash dishes in the kitchen sink.
Daydreaming, allowing myself to think.
I looked up as something caught my eye.
A butcher bird was watching me.
It sat on the window ledge.
Looking in

Another day, another room
A window once again
The butcher bird had found me.
We exchanged looks.
I marvelled at the intelligence.
That little bird displayed.

A silent understanding passed between us.
We may not look the same.
But we are friends,
With things in common.
He came to ask for food.
I gave a helping hand.

He flew away to who knows where.
To come another day
Until he had enough from me
Then another window
Would reflect his presence.
For a new request.

Rock n Roll

Dancing to the music
Jiving to the band
Listening to the Beatles sing
"I want to hold your hand".
Rocking and a rolling
Round the dancehall floor
When the song is over
Hollering for more.

Loving every minute
Not wanting to go home.
Dancing with new people
Not knowing where they're from,
It doesn't really matter,
Nobody really cares,
Just take a chance
And dance, dance, dance.

Vertigo

The room is spinning, and I haven't had a drink.
My head feels explosive.
I cannot even think.
I just feel ill.
Let me be.

I pray it will soon be over.
Till then I will lie still
My head is under cover.
So that I cannot see
The spiralling vortex.

My Pain

Why do you come to give me shocking news?
Does it amuse you to see my pain.
If so, it has been in vain,
I won't show you how I really feel,
That is for me alone.
To know.

If I trusted you, I might reveal.
The remnants of my shattered soul,
I might even give it all.
If I thought you could take it,
What then for you and me
If I told you.

I'm not alone in feeling pain,
How I process it is unique,
So do not try to seek.
A way forward unless I offer.
To let you in to my world
Of solitude.

The Three Wise Gum Trees

Three squiggly gums stand proudly in the sun,
I see them all, then one by one,
I marvel at the majesty, the beauty,
The wisdom held within their core.
If only I could hear it.

The bark long gone.
Peeled off and fallen to the ground,
The branches and leaves resplendent.
With the sound of birds and insects
And creatures of the night.

I wonder what memories you hold.
Of all that you have witnessed,
Do you even have memories?
Of all the lives you've seen
Come and go.

Are you part of my world, or am I part of yours?
You stand in my garden, yet I own you not,
I thank you for your great stature.
Teaching me to stand tall.
Proudly, boldly.

The Power of Nature

Growing in the crack in the concrete
A violet flower flourished,
It didn't complain the lack of room,
It grew all the same.

The sun smiled warmly upon it,
Its little leaves so healthy and green
I think this little flower,
Is the most beautiful I've seen.

The power of nature is impressive,
Giving pleasure to those that see
With eyes of gracious wonder
The gift to you and me.

Empty Head

Sometimes I sit to write.
And my mind is empty.
Nothing is forthcoming.
Just when I need it pumping.

The mind is such a fickle thing.
I can't seem to control it.
When I want it quiet it chatters
About nothing that really matters

I will sit here a little longer
To see if anything comes.
My fingers will be ready.
To type it fast and steady

No, nothing is happening.
I will have a cup of tea.
Then I'll come back later.
When my mind is behaving better.

Words

Words are powerful when they are read,
sometimes more so when they are said,
different meaning when heard,
some words are fun, others absurd.

Discombobulate is a favourite of mine,
it makes me smile and I'm inclined,
to laugh aloud and give a snort,
then there are words I like to quote.

Some words are simply a joy to hear.
Others can evoke fear,
but then there are those,
that can curl your toes.

So be aware of what you say and write.
Speak with love rather than spite,
Once out of your mouth it is too late,
Better to first contemplate.

Think first then before you speak.
Let your words be strong not weak,
Say what you mean whilst being kind.
Let your mouth coordinate with your mind.

The Beach

I watched the man from a distance,
he was standing still at the edge of the water,
at the beach,
I wondered what he was thinking,
As he gazed out to sea.

I almost felt intrusive,
watching his private moments,
He looked over his shoulder,
As if he could sense me there,
Did he see me looking at him?

I hoped he was okay,
That he was simply taking in the view,
The day was far too beautiful for any kind of tragedy.
I left him on the beach as I walked away,
I guess I will never know for sure,
What he was doing there.

Hope

Hope was strong in my heart,
For a good outcome, in a bad situation,
But who was I to determine what fate should be,
One that would satisfy me.

Life brings so many challenges,
Some good, some not,
Letting go would be easy,
If I wasn’t so invested in outcomes.

The Old Man

The old man sat in his armchair which was nearly as worn as he.
It was snowing outside but it would soon turn to ice.
There was a small heater doing its best to heat the cold room.
The man had a rug over his arthritic knees.
He was alone, his wife died several years ago.
He wasn't used to the loneliness yet even though years had passed.
The empty chair opposite his reminded him daily of her absence.
It had once been filled with her loving presence.

He had known love and given love in return but that was so long ago,
All he had now were photographs to help him recall those loved filled days.
His neighbours were young and busy.
His life was empty now and he longed for the day that he could join his wife.
His appetite was small, the days were long and the nights fretful,
He never really knew what day it was, there were no visitors to remind him.

One day as he sat in his armchair, he thought he saw images of his wife beckoning him,
He was overjoyed and eager to go with her,
He didn't care where, just that they were together again,
His breathing had been laboured of late,
Each breath harder than the next,
He let out one long last breath, to go with her.

The Nursing Home

The rooms were small, they contained a bed, a chair and
odds and ends of memorabilia,
A woman was staring at the wall in her room,
I walked by and felt a stab of sorrow,
As I felt her loneliness.

A man came out of his room,
He had dementia, confusion written boldly on his face.
Not really knowing where he was,
I felt a stab of sorrow,
For his lost memories.

I decided then and there, that when I get older,
I will do my best to stay fit and active,
So that no one will feel a stab of sorrow,
At a life once lived.

Tears

Tears formed in the corner of her eyes,
Ready to cascade into the abyss of grief.
There they would join a thousand heartaches and shattered dreams.
Broken promises, endless it seemed, on the road to hell.
Would she survive the trial by fire,
Out of the ashes will her phoenix rise.?
Or will she be swallowed deep in the underbelly of darkness.
Is the world a better place without her,
Or will her survival and liberation serve others,
As she emerges stronger, wiser, victorious.

A Winters Day

The wind was howling, blowing a gale,
It made older people feel small and frail,
Better off inside.

Those that had to go out,
Had to yell and shout,
To be heard.

Spring still months from now,
People wondering how,
To get by.

Plants underground,
Waiting for the sound,
To come forth.

Who Are You

Who are you? I asked the image in the mirror,
The face looked familiar but more lined than I remembered,
Remnants of a life gone by, reflected.
The skin looser and not as alive as it once was,
Yet I could see the light behind the eyes,
Full of memories and experiences.

The same face seen differently day by day,
Sometimes an inner youth appears with impish smile,
Reminding me that though the face may be older now,
The spirit of the eternal ageless me,
Is there for me to see,
When I get past the judgement
Of how my look should be.

Insight

I looked upon you with fresh eyes,
I saw a beauty not seen before,
I recognised you as my true self,
The self I longed to be.
I didn't know the way before,
To find you in the depths,
I always looked outside myself,
For the me I thought I was,
Now I know I am not the one,
Who thinks both day and night,
But rather that I am the source,
Of knowing and awareness.

The Enemy Within

I heard a voice, it said "The enemy is within",
I knew then that the world I carried on my shoulders,
Had nothing to do with outside myself,
It was the emotional baggage,
A heavy load,
Inside.

I was grateful that the voice had pointed the way,
For me to heal my worries and anxieties,
I may not have been fully ready,
But I knew now how to begin,
Where to start,
Inside.

The Ceiling of my Mind

The ceiling of my mind was blown today,
New thoughts and ideas outside the parameters of normal,
I touched the universe,
I saw the truth, revealed in a glorious moment,
I almost know who I am,
Where I come from and where I am going.
I have heard of such revelations,
Experienced by others, some gone before,
Some here and now, my peers,
Showing the way
To ecstasy
Without drugs.

The Human Condition

We laugh, we cry, we live, we die,
We have wants and needs, have different creeds,
We love and hate, our feelings abate,
Then rise again.
We mourn our loss, celebrate our gains,
We love our children, hurt with their pains,
Introvert, extrovert, matters not,
It is all the human condition.

The Man That You Have Become

Though I see the little boy with sparkling eyes
And giggles loud and clear
You stand before me now
As the man that you have become.

I see with love the maturity and the wisdom,
Won by battles of the mind,
The ups and downs of living,
Brought you to the man you have become.

My heart is filled with wonder,
That you passed along my way
And that in some small way,
I have added to the man you have become.

Head and Heart

My head and heart say different things,
My head is clouded by thoughts of all description,
My heart feels the emotions long held tightly,
Too deep to be expressed verbally,
In case the flood gates open
And I drown.

Yet I need to face the depth with courage,
And if I drown, perhaps I will die and be reborn,
A newer and better version of myself,
One in which the keys to wisdom,
Unlock the doors to love,
And I live.

Death Beside Me

The old lady is 91yrs old,
Her mind is dimmed with forgetfulness,
Yet she remembers the oddest things,
And repeats them as if for the first time.

Her garden is overgrown,
But she never steps outside,
In her mind it is still her special place,
I do not tell her how it really is.

I see death in her eyes, waiting,
For her body to let go and release her spirit,
Yet part of her still clings to life, hopeful,
Perhaps another few years, perhaps another few months,
Death has its own timetable.

The Garden

I see you withering in the winter cold,
Some of you seem to be dead,
And yet I know that in spring,
You will again raise your little heads,
And smile upon the world
My world.

The birds will walk amongst you,
Looking for their daily food,
I will again watch with wonder,
At how their antics lift my mood,
And I will smile upon the world,
Your world.

The Mist

The mist rolled in over the water,
Giving it a mystical look and feel,
It transported me to Avalon
And the lady of the lake.

For a short while I saw Arthur
and the knights of the round table,
my mind enchanted as if by Merlin
and his magic.

I imagined Camelot in the distance,
The great hall and its enormous fireplace,
Then a passerby brought me back to reality
And reluctantly I left it all behind.

He

His wounds weren't visible on the outside,
They lay hidden in the depths of his being,
Life had shown him the worst aspects of itself.

He couldn't verbalise them or even process them,
In fact, he wasn't even sure of what he had seen,
Yet he had lived through it.

His mind had this habit of questioning the validity,
Was what he had seen even true,
Or was he trapped in some nightmare.

Nights were not kind, days not much better,
He longed to be free of it all,
To be at peace.

She

Her heart had been broken more than once,
She tried to gather up the pieces,
And glue them back together.

She knew that her experience wasn't hers alone,
Many others had felt the same anguish and pain,
Yet that was no comfort.

Only time would offer reconstruction,
Of the shattered emotions,
And the promise of better times.

We

Together we can bring change, if we agree,
That change needs to be made.
Some are hungry for different ways,
Others happy with what they know.

Change is challenging and to some frightening,
The unknown, unpredictable future we face,
A step too far, for now.
We are not yet united.

Will it ever be that we agree to move forward,
One for all and all for one,
Or will ego, doubt, and fear,
Keep us bound.

The Little Girl

The little girl cried,
When told that she had lied,
When she had not.

She grew in height,
She woke in fright,
From nightmares.

In adult years,
There were some tears,
At life.

As she grew old,
She became quite bold,
Her head held high.

When death came,
Her life to claim,
She calmly went.

Man and Boy

The man carries a wounded, traumatised boy inside,
Sometimes the boy cries out for love and safety,
Other times the man takes the place of the scared child.

The man doesn't know how to love himself enough,
To give the boy the feeling that he is treasured,
The struggle arises when he feels threatened and alone.

I want to hold that man/boy,
And tell him that I care, I want him to feel safe,
That he is loved and that I am here.

Her Fragrance

The smell of her perfume lingered on his clothes,
He remembered the embrace,
The thrill of having her close.
He couldn't wait until he saw her again,
But until then he would fill himself,
With the memory of that afternoon.

Intense love and longing filled him,
He was a little surprised at the depth of emotion,
He hadn't felt quite this way before,
He knew she was the one,
His forever sweet love.

The Storm

First came the heavy rain,
Followed by the thunder and lightning,
Dogs barked, cats cowered,
It was so severe.

The thud of raindrops on the rooftop,
Signalled what was to come,
Batten down the hatches
Everyone.

The plants in the garden
At first welcomed the downpour,
Then I could see them withering
Almost drowned.

It seemed to last for hours,
With no promise of respite
Then just as quickly as it came,
It left us in the night.

Forgiveness

Forgive me he said, I have wronged you,
His words fell on deaf ears,
Forgive me he said,
I thought of all the tears,
That I had shed.

Forgive you, how can I, I said,
You tore my world in two,
Nothing left but rubble,
To rebuild anew,
My life.

In time, I forgave,
Not for him, but for me,
I couldn't carry him around any longer,
I needed to be free,
To live.

Memories

Little birds darted here and there from branch to branch on
the tree outside.
Next the parrots with their bright attire, vivid in the sun,
I watched them for a while, then the old willow tree with its
rope swing caught my eye.
I remembered the children playing for hours on it.
I felt a little sad that the time had gone,
When laughter filled the air.

I was old now, only memories carried me through the days,
The nights filled with broken sleep,
Each day, each night, just the same,
Even the memories were sketchy at times,
But when I looked out at the world that used to be,
In a way it comforted me.

The Shed

The shed out back,
Filled with stuff,
Hardly ever used these days,
Gone is the need to use them.
No more grass to mow.

The spiders love the shed,
A dry place to weave their webs,
Away from birds that love to eat them,
I guess I will leave the shed,
Alone.

Today

Enjoy today, and think not of tomorrow,
It may bring happiness, it may bring sorrow,
No time like the present.
It is only Now that matters,
We can't control the rest,
Though we do our best
To keep control of life.

The Voice in My Head

You have been wronged in the past
Said the voice in my head,
Why hang on to pain, making it last,
Let go and be free.

I've tried and I've tried,
The same voice cried,
Which voice will I listen to,
In my head.

Why struggle and doubt,
I'll throw that voice out,
I'll choose the voice of reason,
And be free.

The News

I watched the news, what a mistake,
Nothing but tragedy and misfortune,
If only they would say,
Something uplifting today,
I wouldn't have to change the channel.

With serious face and lowered voice,
The latest catastrophe reported,
The presenter tells us the latest horror,
Not much better news tomorrow,
I'll bet.

Perhaps I will be a rebel,
And not watch the news again
Over dinner at night,
Fright after morbid fright,
Takes its toll.

Surely there is more to the world,
Than the news of the day,
I will make up my own,
And totally disown,
Anything other than good news.

The Lie

What is a lie,
Other than a distortion of the truth?
It is an arrow that pierces the heart,
When found out.

What is a lie,
Other than words turned inside out?
It is a betrayal of trust,
A deliberate act.

What is a lie,
That comes out of your mouth.
It is emotional abuse of another,
To save yourself.

The Piano Player

His fingers dexterous on the keys,
Gliding expertly back and forth,
The music soothed my soul,
I wondered how he felt.
As he created such harmony,
With his hands.

Was his own soul touched,
By the creation of such beauty?
Did his mind dissolve
As he becomes one with the notes,
Lost in the moment.

For a short time
I melded with his essence,
As we became one,
He the musician, me the receiver,
Unified by the sound.

The Daffodils

The daffodils, so beautiful
In their simple yellow robes,
Such joy and radiance
Flows out from their cheery smiles,
They lift my soul.
From earth to heaven.

I arrange them in a vase.
Uplifting the room with simplicity,
Yet such a peaceful countenance
Exudes from each flower head,
My heart beats more evenly
As I look at natures gift.

Spammers and Scammers

Spam, spam, scam after scam,
Where do these people come from,
They prey on the aged and the vulnerable,
They hope we will fall for there lies,
And give them access to all our money.

Blacklist and block are the only recourse,
Our walls of defences strengthened,
We must be aware,
That scammers will share,
Our details with more spammers and scammers.

Heart of My Heart

Heart of my heart,
Love of my life,
My soul searched for you,
Amongst the crowd.
When I saw you, I almost didn't recognise,
That you were the one
I longed for.
You spoke to me.
With words that pierced the armour
I had moulded to my vulnerable heart,
Then I saw that you were the one,
That I had been looking for.

Magical View

I looked upon the world today,
With eyes anew
Even though I saw the same images,
They somehow seemed more magical.
It seemed that today I saw through my heart,
And saw things that aren't visible to the eyes,
And a stirring began,
A new respect and wonder
For the world in which I live.
There was an aliveness to all,
Even those things that looked to have no soul,
Life is life no matter how small,
It may be.

The Waterfall

The noise and water spray was inconceivable.
Until I experienced it for myself,
I had put my ideas and judgments on the shelf.
Of things no longer needed.
I marvelled at the power and majesty,
Much greater than my own
Yet.
Perhaps one day I will identify and accept,
that which is within me and us all,
then I will be as wonderful
as that mighty waterfall.

The Café

A small skinny decaf cappuccino I said,
My usual every week.
I loved the café vibe,
Where strangers would speak
To each other.
We had our own table for sure,
We were a community of tea and coffee lovers,
We chose this café above all the others,
Because friends could meet, and strangers greet,
With a smile and a nod to each other.

Nature Spirits

The fairies danced, the little elves pranced,
In their garden home full of plants.
The trees sheltered homes,
And little people's domes,
Where merriment was the main factor.
The bees played their part,
They took it to heart,
To do their bit for the flowers,
And colourful wings glowed,
The loveliness showed,
With the sun on their backs,
Little feet tracks,
A garden of Eden for all.

Little Dog Big Dog

The little dog yelped,
The big dog barked,
The little one ran,
The big one sprang,
Into action.

The little one bled,
I knew it was dead,
The big one was strong,
It didn't need long,
To kill.

I was feeling quite sad,
That the big dog was bad,
The little one had no defence,
The owner could receive no recompense,
For her loss.

The call of the wild,
Though seemingly mild,
Takes over when least expected,
The wild nature cannot be detected,
In time.

The Rhythm of Life

I am in no doubt,
That my life throughout,
Has been filled with lessons galore.
I hope that I've learnt,
That the wisdom I've earned,
Is worth every tear that I shed.
The good times and bad,
Are happy and sad,
They had made the Me of today.
I can't change a thing,
I think I'll just sing,
In tune with life's melody.

Here's To You

Wherever you are,
Whatever you do,
My thoughts and best wishes are yours.
Whether working away,
Or staying at home doing chores,
I send you, all my love,
Our hopes and our dreams,
Though separate it seems,
Are really one and the same.

We are at the end of book now and I hope that within these pages you have found a poem that resonates just for you. Though we share many feelings we each experience life a little differently. I have tried to include a variety of poems that reflect the diversity of life and the depth of my inner world.

Connie Howell 2023

About Connie Howell

Connie Howell is the author of several books and is a poet who lives in the Blue Mountains, West of Sydney, Australia. Her book, *Perfectly Imperfect, how to be imperfect and remain lovable*, published by Deep Read Press, was nominated for the 2022 Writers' Lounge Bookshelf Award.

Thoughts of a Wounded Healer is her second book of verse. Like her first book of verse, *Soul Deep*, it reflects her love of expressing the depths of herself through the written word.

British by birth she migrated to Australia in 1973 and it is here that she became an author. However, in her youth while at senior school she began writing poetry but never kept a record of any of her poems.

You can find Connie on social media and on her website www.conniehowell.com.au

www.ingramcontent.com/pod-product-compliance
Lightning Source LLC
LaVergne TN
LVHW010121170826
845678LV00012B/2530

* 9 7 8 1 9 5 4 9 8 9 3 5 1 *